FINANCIAL ADVISORS ATTRACT THEIR Ideal Clients WITH A Book

11 Ways Financial Advisors Attract Their Ideal Clients with a Book

HOW TO STAND OUT IN A CROWDED MARKET AND DRAMATICALLY DIFFERENTIATE YOURSELF AS THE AUTHORITY, CELEBRITY AND EXPERT

ADAM WITTY

Published by Advantage, Charleston, South Carolina.
Member of Advantage Media Group.

ADVANTAGE is a registered trademark and the Advantage colophon is a trademark of Advantage Media Group, Inc.

Printed in the United States of America.

ISBN: 978-159932-454-8
LCCN: 2013951018

Advantage Media Group is proud to be a part of the Tree Neutral® program. Tree Neutral offsets the number of trees consumed in the production and printing of this book by taking proactive steps such as planting trees in direct proportion to the number of trees used to print books. To learn more about Tree Neutral, please visit **www.treeneutral.com**. To learn more about Advantage's commitment to being a responsible steward of the environment, please visit **www.advantagefamily.com/green**

YOUR OPPORTUNITY TO ACHIEVE MORE

Do you want more from your business? More income? More clients you enjoy working with? Do you want to make more of an impact? Do you want to share your stories, passion, and knowledge with more of the world?

Your opportunity to accomplish all of this—and more—is here.

Throughout my career, I have had the great fortune to work with hundreds of people from nearly every type of business, and every walk of life. Entrepreneurs, small-business owners, professional speakers, attorneys, doctors, financial advisors, mortgage brokers, insurance and annuity specialists, philanthropists—the list goes on.

The Advantage Media Group team and I have helped each person move from business professional to author. I've watched them take their businesses to the next level, grow their income, and expand their reach by being the authority, celebrity, and expert in their field. I've shared their elation when they hold a copy of their book for the first time.

Most importantly, I have had the great satisfaction of knowing our authors are doing what they've always dreamed of and are moving ahead to accomplish even more.

That is the power of a book.

Today, as we move into a new and very different economy, this magical power of a book is more important than ever. To achieve success, you must be dramatically different and stand apart from the pack. You must be very clear on the value you offer, matching your services and philosophies to the clients you want to attract. You must be recognized as a thought leader. And you must genuinely earn your clients' support.

In the pages ahead, you will meet 11 financial advisors and other professionals who have published a book. You'll discover how they use books to build their business and change their lives. Yes, you will have to invest time and money, both while creating your book, and in marketing your book after it is published. But as you will soon read, this investment in your business, your message, and yourself is worth every minute—and every penny.

Imagine the possibilities. Then go for it. There is no time like now.

To Your Success,

Adam D. Witty
Founder & Chief Executive Officer
Advantage Media Group

TABLE OF CONTENTS

AND ACCESS FREE RESOURCES FOR POTENTIAL AUTHORS!

It doesn't matter where you are in the world, Adam can help you share your Stories, Passion, and Knowledge with the world in the form of a published book.

Visit HOWTOATTRACTIDEALCLIENTS.COM/REGISTER to access these free resources:

RECEIVE a subscription to the Author Success University™ monthly teleseminar wherein successful authors and book marketing experts reveal their tips and tricks for marketing and growing a business with a book

REGISTER for a webinar led by Adam Witty: "How to Quickly Write, Publish, And Profit From A Book That Will Grow Your Business"

COMPLETE Advantage's Publishing Questionnaire and receive a complimentary Discovery Call with an acquisitions editor to help you determine if your ideas, concepts, or manuscript are worth turning into a book

ACCESS ALL OF THE ABOVE FREE RESOURCES BY REGISTERING YOUR BOOK AT

HOWTOATTRACTIDEALCLIENTS.COM/REGISTER

FOREWORD

How to Create an Extraordinary Business

by Matt Zagula

Master Coach to Elite Financial Advisors

FOREWORD

How to Create an Extraordinary Business

by Matt Zagula

Master Coach to Elite Financial Advisors

I am assuming you are here today because you're tired of the status quo.

You're probably really good at what you do. You likely offer premium financial advisory services. And you know you can generate tremendous value for your clients.

Yet if no one else knows, your talents will never matter.

Right now, you're one small fish in a sea of financial advisors. Your prospects can choose any one of them. From their viewpoint, you might as well be invisible. And, unfortunately, most financial advisors will remain this way. In part, this is due to the competition. More importantly, many financial advisors miss the real reason why people want to work with them. As a result, they continue using the same old marketing techniques with lackluster results.

You see, people who come to financial advisors are searching. They often feel their financial future is out of their control in an economic system they seldom understand. They need more than promises or a list of services. They need someone they can *trust*.

For most people, stock market predictions, bond yields, even their advisor's recommendations, have little meaning. Many don't understand this information, although they can get it from just about any advisor. However, what they can understand is their financial advisor's philosophy. They can relate to your core values and connect with your world view.

This is what you need to provide in your book. Your personality and beliefs are the elements that create trust. And they are the reasons why your ideal clients will want to work with *you*.

Ultimately, your book is not going to convince *everybody* that you're the right choice. Rather, it serves to create a message that expresses your belief system. So, when your prime consumers can read your words and say, "I totally agree with this," you'll know your book has accomplished far more than any other marketing you've done before.

Before you have a book to call your own, you often hunt for ice-cold prospects and push your services. You try to appeal to everyone, yet feel like just a number—or worse, isolated from the people you want to reach. You work hard and strive for success but can barely get by in this tough economic climate.

After a book, you are an authority on your topic. You no longer need to search for prospects. Your positioning in the market draws prospects to you. They arrive at your door because they feel as if they already know you and because they agree with your philosophies. You can now appeal to the market you can benefit most. And you feel as if you are part of something bigger, a force that can truly help people.

You still work hard, but now your efforts are focused. Instead of just getting by, you enjoy your most prosperous year ever. Better yet, *striving for success* becomes *fulfilling your dreams.*

In this book, you will find the stories of 11 financial advisors who are now authors. They are scattered across the US. Some serve unique niche markets. Yet all have faced the same challenges you are experiencing now.

You will read how they have turned businesses around —even upside down. They'll share how they use books to attract top prospects, increase referrals, and create new business opportunities. More importantly, they'll tell you how, as recognized authorities, they have increased their incomes and transformed their lives.

The most important thing to know is you can do the same. Your message in a book, written with a clear goal in mind, *will* transform your business. As my friend and business partner, Dan Kennedy, once said, "It's more than sharing your message. It's writing a book with a purpose, and then marketing it with a strategy."

If you're tired of feeling in a rut with your business or doing just "OK"—it's time to get started. Contact Advantage Media Group. They will help you determine a purpose, fine-tune your message, and develop a strategy. They will guide you through your manuscript or make it easy to write with a unique program that allows you to talk your book. Either way, your book will be polished, professional, *and* strategic.

In the end, you will have the most powerful deliverable in the world: a professionally published book, authored by you.

If you're hesitating, know this: *you will never fail when you make an investment in yourself.* What you gain is ultimate clarity in your vision and business goals. But there is far more on the table than that. This is your opportunity to take your business to the next level. And once you do, you will never look back.

MEET 11 FINANCIAL PROFESSIONALS AND ADVANTAGE AUTHORS WHO ARE BUILDING BUSINESSES—AND CHANGING LIVES—WITH THEIR BOOKS.

CHRIS ABTS

President and Founder, Cornerstone Retirement Services

Author, *Redefining Retirement: Creating Security In An Unsecure World*

Chris decided to write his book because he recognized the importance of establishing authority, celebrity, and exclusivity in his market. "If you're serious about the business or industry that you're in, you've got to be noted as an expert or leader," says Chris. "And a major part of that is done with a book. It opens doors and positions you as an authority figure in your industry or area."

Cornerstone Retirement is located in Reno, Nevada.

www.CornerstoneRetirement.com

JEANNETTE BAJALIA

President and Founder, Petros Estate and Retirement Planning and Woman's Worth®

Author, *Wise Up Women! A Guide to Total Fiscal and Physical Well-Being*

Jeannette founded Woman's Worth® to meet the unique financial needs of single, divorced, and widowed women. She is using her book not only to build her business, but also to share her message: "I want to empower women to take charge of their financial futures with the information I provide."

Jeannette maintains two offices in Jacksonville and St. Augustine, Florida.

www.Womans-Worth.com and

www.PetrosPlanning.com

MIKE CANET

President and Founder, Prostatis Financial Advisors Group

Author, *Surviving the Perfect Storm: How to Create a Financial Plan That Will Withstand Any Crisis*

In addition to establishing trust with clients and prospective clients, Mike says, "it's also nice to be able to say you're a published author." By incorporating his book into strategic marketing, Mike has almost doubled his business over the past two years.

Prostatis Financial Advisors Group is located in Glen Burnie, Maryland.

www.ProstatisAdvisors.com

MATT DICKEN

Founder, Strategic Wealth Designers

Author, *Retirement Planning in a New Direction: A Return to Common Sense*

A book allowed Matt to summarize all of his ideas in one resource for both clients and prospects. "When you hear something, you only retain part of it. But if you can go home and read it again, that reinforces it." His book is now integral to building his business.

Matt's office can be found in Louisville, Kentucky.

www.AskMattDicken.com

BRIAN FRICKE

President, Financial Management Concepts

Author, *Worry Free Retirement: Do What You Want, When You Want, Where You Want*

Brian uses his book to enhance his credibility, strengthen relationships with clients, and generate new leads. His results are "definitely positive" when it comes to his income. Brian recently said, "Finding Advantage Media Group was the best thing that could have happened."

Brian provides advice from his office in Winter Springs, Florida.

www.BrianFricke.com

GREG HAMMOND

President, Hammond Iles Wealth Advisors

Co-author, *You Can Do More That Matters*

Greg, and his co-author, Ron Ware, help individuals and couples meet philanthropic goals. Both believe their book allows them to "reach a much wider audience" in this area. And both were happy to write it with Advantage Media Group. "Ron and I are both process guys," Greg says, "so the idea of writing a book through a process that was executable and easy to plug into, from beginning to end, was very attractive."

Hammond Iles operates in three Connecticut locations: Wethersfield, Old Lyme, and Woodbridge.

www.HammondIles.com

THOMAS HELBIG

Founder and CEO, Retirement Advisory Group

Author, *The Boomer's Guide to a Worry-Free Retirement*

Thomas has reaped several benefits from his book, not the least of which is doubling his income in one year. It's easy to see why he says his book "was the best investment I have ever made."

Thomas is located in St. Louis, Missouri.

www.RetirementKey.com

MARTY HIGGINS

Founder, Family Wealth Management LLC

Author, *Distributionland: A Retiree's Survival Manual for Transitioning to a World of New Rules and Unexpected Dangers*

Marty's main goal for his book is to attract top clients. "Being an author gives you one of the highest levels of credibility, and perception is reality," he says. And as a bonus, he adds, Advantage makes the process "really simple."

Family Wealth Management can be found in Marlton, New Jersey.

www.FamilyWealthAdvisory.com

ANN VANDERSLICE

President and CEO, Federal Retirement Planning Strategies

Author, *FedTelligence: The Ultimate Guide to Mastering Your Federal Benefits*

While Ann was well-known in her local area, she wanted to expand her reputation among federal employees nationally. A book enabled her to do this, and more. "It's been a great way to increase my visibility in the federal market and create extra income," Ann says.

Ann is based in Lakewood, Colorado.

www.AnnVanderslice.com

RON WARE

Founder and President, Wealth Impact Partners

Co-author, *You Can Do More That Matters*

Ron and his co-author, Greg Hammond, discovered something unexpected after writing their book: "It's expanded our horizons big time in terms of not only how we build our core businesses, but also in how we can develop opportunities that are way out of the box for us compared to our traditional world. Quite frankly, we may not have discovered some of these things without the book."

Wealth Impact Partners has locations in Wellesley, Massachusetts, and Warwick, Rhode Island.

www.WealthImpactPartners.com

MATT ZAGULA

Master Coach to Elite Financial Advisors

Co-author, *No B.S. Trust-Based Marketing: The Ultimate Guide to Creating Trust in an Understandably Un-Trusting World* and several other books

Matt developed one of the nation's top financial advisory businesses by using his books to pave the way. He believes professionals should use books in every aspect of their marketing. "A book is the power deliverable in creating authority," he says. "And quite frankly, we use it everywhere." Matt is working with Advantage on his latest book now.

Matt is located in Weirton, West Virginia.

www.MattZagula.com

CHAPTER 1

Be the Expert Prospects Go to First

Increase Your Visibility, Credibility, and Clout with a Book

CHAPTER 1

Be the Expert Prospects Go to First

Increase Your Visibility, Credibility, and Clout with a Book

Have you ever wondered how you can possibly stand out among the crowd and be heard over the noise of your competition?

With more than 300 million folks in the United States, it's easy to feel like a grain of sand on a beach. And it seems like *everyone* these days has websites, blogs, free reports, videos, webinars, free CDs, and more.

Now don't get me wrong, these are important and useful marketing tools, and you *should* use them. But you need something *more* to elevate your financial business above the crowd and make you the logical choice—the "go-to" advisor in your area or niche.

That something is a book authored by *you*.

Think of it this way, while there are over six billion world residents, there are only about three million authors. This means that a published author is in the top 0.05 percent of the global population. How is that for differentiation?

Being an author instantly makes you an expert. It catapults you ahead of "the pack." As an author, you are no longer a "me too."

Take Keith Ayers, for example. Keith is a business consultant, coach, and Advantage author of *Engagement is Not Enough: You Need Passionate Employees to Reach Your Dream.* When he brought his new book home, he received an interesting, yet not surprising, reaction from his daughter:

"When my book first arrived, I took a few copies home and showed one to my then 17-year-old daughter. She said, 'This is weird.' I said, 'Why is it weird?' She said, 'It's just weird that my dad has got a book out.' Her father, in her mind, did not fit into the context of an author. Anytime I meet someone new and they find out that I have a published book, it changes the conversation. From a personal point of view … and a business point of view, having a book has been extremely positive."

Keith is experiencing the phenomenon I call the "author aura." Prospects, clients, and customers see you as more credible than your competitors. You suddenly have elevated status. Why? Well, I like the explanation given by someone you may already know, Dan Kennedy.

Now, you may recognize his name since Dan is the founder of Glazer-Kennedy Insider's Circle, or GKIC. He has at least 20 books in print by now, and is planning to write more. As an author, he has established himself as a thought leader in marketing, copywriting, and business building. Thanks to the "author aura," Dan charges upwards of $100,000, plus royalties, for sales campaigns, while picking and choosing the clients he wants to work with.

As Dan says, "Salespeople have brochures. Experts have books." Short and to the point.

Now, you may be thinking to yourself, "Well I don't need to be *the* expert in my city. My service speaks for itself. Our staff has certified training. Our standards are above par." And I'm sure you can think of additional, similar statements, depending on your situation.

Unfortunately, every time you say this, you can bet *your competition is saying it, too.*

So what are you doing that is different or special? How can you ensure that prospects will choose you over your competition? As a financial advisor, this question is especially important. Like it or not, you own a commoditized business. This makes it even more critical for you to differentiate yourself in overcrowded markets.

A book does the heavy lifting when it comes to differentiation. In addition to giving you the "author aura," a book allows you to speak directly to prospects in your niche. After reading your book, your prospects identify with you. They hear your message and feel they actually *know* you. It's not surprising that you become the logical choice, even when there are several other businesses to choose from.

This is why Marty Higgins, founder of Family Wealth Management LLC, wrote his soon-to-be published book, *Distributionland: A Retiree's Survival Manual for Transitioning to a World of New Rules and Unexpected Dangers.* "Everybody does good work," he writes, "or does the best they can, but you have to differentiate yourself, especially in our commoditized industry where the consumer says, 'Since I can get this anywhere, I just want the cheapest price.' You have to differentiate yourself, or you die. One of the best tools of credibility is having your own published book. Then you become the expert."

Although he's in a different industry, construction risk advisor and Advantage author, Robert Phelan, knows this well. His book, *Broke: The Broken Contractors Insurance System and How to Fix It,* is the marketing tool that sets him apart from competition in the insurance industry. As he says, "Insurance is a commodity and a boring commodity at that. My book is a conversation starter, a point of differentiation, and a credibility and expertise builder that has gotten me into the C-suites of prospective clients."

Books work so well because valuable information establishes trust and credibility. This is vital in the financial services industry, according to Matt Dicken. As the founder of Strategic Wealth Designers, he knows how difficult it can be to connect with clients, especially when your audience is broad. "In our business, individuals are often very confused as far as what to do," he says. "They're really looking for someone who is a true authority. There's a lot of noise out there from various companies or advisors and people really struggle to see who they should believe or trust. Anybody can have an opinion, but when you're the person who wrote the book, you're viewed as somebody that is different from an average advisor."

Founder and CEO of the Retirement Advisory Group, Thomas Helbig, agrees: "A book definitely motivates new clients. I think it's the trust and credibility. They see me in a different light."

Unlike many financial advisors, Ann Vanderslice has a very specific niche. As the President and CEO of Federal Retirement Planning Strategies, you instantly know the audience she serves. However, while Ann was well-known among federal employees in the Colorado area, she wanted to expand nationally. In just one year, her book has "definitely accomplished this."

In today's ever-changing world, one thing is clear: consumers no longer settle for average service or the best price. They simply have too many choices. Being an author makes you different. You exceed expectations of both prospects and clients because you have gone the extra mile. I think Dan Kennedy sums it up best: "In the professional category, you really want a mix. You want celebrity. You want credibility. You want trust. You want authority. You want expert status. You want differentiation from others. Your book can make a major contribution to every one of those objectives."

At Advantage, we can help you publish a book that positions you as the first choice in your city or financial niche.

Contact us at **advantagefamily.com/finance** to begin. Yes, writing a book takes some effort, but it will pay off for you—time and time again.

CHAPTER 2

Create Loyal Clients and Watch Your Profits Grow

How a Book Fosters Dedication and Enthusiasm—and Turns Clients into Fans

CHAPTER 2

Create Loyal Clients and Watch Your Profits Grow

How a Book Fosters Dedication and Enthusiasm—and Turns Clients into Fans

When Thomas Helbig wrote his book, he never thought it would put him in the league of the world's most powerful companies. After all, when you think of the most successful businesses today, what comes to mind? Apple? Amazon? Or, if you're a die-hard online shopper, Zappos?

However, by publishing a book, Thomas employed the same client-building techniques used by these multi-national corporations. And by using these techniques, *Thomas doubled his business in one year.* To see the connection, let's step back and take a closer look at the corporations I just mentioned.

First, consider what these companies have in common. Of course, great products would be one factor. Superb service, another. In fact, Zappos states, loud and clear, "Powered by Service" right in their logo. You can probably name more commonalities, but all would point to one, overriding characteristic. Each company has a fanatical customer base. They are true fans who not only buy products, they also shout from the rooftops, praising the company to anyone who will listen.

The most profitable companies in the world boast the most fanatical clients and customers. In fact, there is a direct correlation between fanatical clients and profit. Apple, for example, reported a record-setting net profit of $13.06 billion in the first quarter of 2012. Amazon came in at $13.2 billion, above analysts' expectations.

Now, a company builds a fanatical customer base in two main ways:

1. Every action the company takes revolves around a mission to serve the customer *first*.
2. The company is very clear about *communicating* this mission to its audience.

Zappos, for example, goes well beyond stating customer service standards on its website. The company has several blogs with topics ranging from fashion culture to messages from the "Zappos family" along with an Expo site "dedicated to showcasing the innovative work happening at Zappos." Their reason for communicating this way is simple. By providing more information, they deliver more value to the customer. They are creating a "family" and customers want to be a part of it.

There is another benefit to providing information beyond establishing a connection with your clients. For financial advisors, helpful content makes it more likely your clients will succeed with your investment advice. Clear and detailed information results in understanding. You also develop a relationship with prospects and clients, especially when you let your personality show. Trust deepens. As a result, they are far more likely to comply with your instructions. They go beyond the point of being good clients to becoming true fans.

At this point, you may be making the connection from global corporation to local financial advisor. Thomas explains it this way: "It helps them to become a better client. Maybe they're more relaxed. Maybe they trust me more. But my advice just makes sense to them, and it's really grown my business as a result."

Stronger client relationships are important to Brian Fricke as well. Shortly after releasing his book, the President of Financial Management Concepts gave a copy to every client. He had an important reason for doing this: "Clients can get a flavor of who I am and our philosophies. Therefore, it tends to create a stronger bond between the two of us."

Matt Dicken published *Retirement Planning in a New Direction: A Return to Common Sense*, in part, to reinforce the advice he gives his clients. "When you hear something, you only retain part of it," he says. "But if you can go back home and read it again, well that reinforces it. So, I wanted a resource where all of my ideas could be in one place where clients, or potential clients, can go back and read through it several times."

Ann Vanderslice couldn't agree more. As she says, "federal benefits are a complicated topic. And because of that complexity, I need to break it down into simple terms. My book is written just like I speak, so when people want to go back and review, it's easy for them to do. They'll often tell me, 'this sounds just like you.' So, I know it works."

A book is one of the best tools to reinforce your viewpoints and message. And by sharing your beliefs, you create the glue that bonds you with your prospects and clients. However, there is yet another way you can use a book to benefit both your clients and your business.

THE UNEXPECTED BENEFIT OF A GIFT—FOR YOU AND YOUR CLIENTS

Let's go back to our multinational corporations again. These companies use another technique that helps to grow a passionate fan base: a systematic plan to show appreciation to customers.

Now think for a moment about all of the companies that have sent you gifts in appreciation for your business. That didn't take very long, did it? Few businesses do this. And because few businesses do, this is an even greater reason why *you should*. It is an easy way to stand out among your competitors.

Naturally, this raises the question, what do I give? Why not a copy of your book? Books are fabulous client gifts for an important reason. As a society, we place a high value on books. It may be $15, $20, even $50, depending on the book, but we attach a price to it. So when someone gives us a book, we read it, add it to our library, or share it with a friend. It goes well beyond the free information you can find just about anywhere today.

A book is an important tool in any sound client-appreciation system. Giving your book to clients communicates thoughtfulness on your part. It also provides a platform for your message, beliefs, and for *you*. It strengthens your connection with clients, making you a valued part of their lives.

Coach, speaker, and Advantage author Chris Ruisi experienced this benefit by sharing his book, *Step Up and Play Big*, with clients. Since then, several of those readers have joined others in giving his book glowing reviews on Amazon. The gift not only allows Chris to further his relationship with his clients, but it also allows him to promote his book at the same time.

Mike Canet, President of Prostatis Financial Advisors Group, gives his clients a signed book, as well as extras to give away. His clients win, and so does Mike because, as he notes, “It keeps a consistent referral base coming in.”

At Advantage, we can help you find your unique message and create your fan base with a book. You may not have as many fans as Apple, but they *will* help you grow your business. Take the first step by contacting us at **advantagefamily.com/finance**.

CHAPTER 3

An Easy Way to Get New Clients Who Are Five Times More Valuable to Your Business

Increase Your Quantity and Quality of Referrals with a Book

CHAPTER 3

An Easy Way to Get New Clients Who Are Five Times More Valuable to Your Business

Increase Your Quantity and Quality of Referrals with a Book

Did you know there is an easy, yet often overlooked, method for acquiring new clients? And what if I told you these new clients will, on average, spend *five times* more with your business than a client you acquire through general marketing or advertising?

This gold mine of new clients comes from *referrals*. As a financial advisor, you're likely not surprised. The most profitable businesses report that well over 70 percent of new clients result from referrals made by current clients. Financial advisor and author of several books, Matt Zagula, notes that "In most professional services and even in most businesses, a referral to a high-value client is sort of the nirvana of business."

So why are referred clients so valuable?

When prospects arrive to your business from referrals, they are essentially pre-sold. A referral from a friend or family member validates that you and your business are the real deal. Your new prospect believes you'll do everything you say you will, and then some. They arrive at your business with a sense of trust, even respect. They are much easier to convince, they are ready to buy, and they are willing to spend more money.

As a rule of thumb, studies show that roughly 20 percent of your clients will freely give referrals without you asking. Another 20 percent will not give referrals at all. So that leaves 60 percent of your clients who will likely refer you and your business if you ask them, or equally important, if you make it easy to do.

Dan Kennedy once remarked that getting a referral has a great deal to do with how people feel about the professional they are referring. People like to give referrals when they can brag at a cocktail party or tell others, "My advisor wrote the book on retirement funding." As Dan says, "A book can create a referral process that enhances the status of the customer facilitating the referral, rather than diminishing it, thereby making it easier for them to do it."

Nearly every Advantage author has increased referrals to their business with their book and grown their income as a result. And they've done it both online and offline. Now, online referrals often occur from person to person through social media. But the rubber *really* hits the road when an online guru with a strong, loyal following endorses your book. Think about it. If you agree with someone's philosophies, you are more apt to follow their recommendations. Their endorsement is often just as strong as one provided by a friend. In addition, their referral reaches thousands of people at one time. Talk about benefiting your business!

Advantage author Pat Williams uses this strategy to promote his books with great success. Now, any sports fan will likely recognize Pat's name since he is the co-founder of the Orlando Magic basketball team. He currently has at least 65 books and is planning to write more. Pat explains it this way, "Get books into the hands of chatterboxes. If you can get the army of cheerleaders talking about your book, or tweeting, or emailing, that's the ultimate."

Offline referrals are just as effective and, in my opinion, even easier to get. An easy way to start is to give copies of your book to clients, and then ask them to pass a copy along to friends, family, and colleagues. The book instantly creates a "conversation starter" for your clients when they talk with friends. In essence, you have greased the skids, making it easier—even prestigious—for your clients to give referrals, just as Dan mentioned above.

Matt Zagula has honed his referral system to a fine art. He gives new clients a copy of his book as well as his *Consumer's Guide to Finding the Right Advice Giver*. He then asks clients to tell friends, family members, or neighbors because "These are the people that we like and trust." For Matt, referrals are vital to his practice. As he says, "It's worked better than anything else we've ever done to attract new business."

There are several creative ways to share your book with clients and prospective clients. Jeannette Bajalia is the President of both Petros Estate and Retirement Planning and Woman's Worth. She leaves copies in the reception areas of her two office locations. Her partner, Brian Mickley, made this observation, "You see people picking it up and they start leafing through it. When it's time for their appointment, many will set it down saying, 'Oh, I'd really like to read that.' This gives us a wonderful opportunity to surprise them when they leave. Our Client Relations person will say, 'I noticed you were interested in Jeannette's book. Here's your copy to take home to read and then give to someone else.'"

Imagine the pleasure of receiving an unexpected gift like this. It's a wonderful way to build relationships, in addition to encouraging referrals.

Brian Fricke experiences this, as well. He gives every client two copies of his book and asks they pass one on to any friends or family members who might need his help. Brian also enjoys another benefit from client referrals made this way. He tells me that, thanks to his book, referred prospects are more qualified and ready to work with him. "One chapter in the book is titled 'If I Ran the Country for a Day.' In it, I rant and rave and give people a sense of me. I know it attracts people because they have commented on it. But I'm sure it turns people off, too. But that's OK. It saves time for everybody."

This has certainly been Matt Dicken's experience. He once told me that his book can turn a "lukewarm lead" into a "hot lead *before* they meet with me. If I can get them to read the book before they meet with me, it makes the appointment with them much more productive and successful because I don't have to spend 20 or 30 minutes trying to build credibility and explaining what I do. The book has already done that for me."

This leads me to the second slam-dunk when it comes to using your book for referrals. With a book, you have more control over the message your clients share. Although your clients may love doing business with you, this does not guarantee they'll deliver your "30-second commercial" in good form. In fact, your best clients may be driving prospects away by saying the wrong things . . . unintentionally. However, with a book, you can often make up for these mistakes. Your book is your scripted masterpiece; the same masterpiece your referrals will read. It virtually guarantees that potential clients will get the exact message you want them to hear.

Some financial planners try to boost referrals by offering incentives. While this may encourage clients to give the referral, it does not guarantee they will correctly deliver your message. However, when your client delivers your book the helpful information inside overcomes this obstacle. Plus, the book makes it easy for your clients to strike up a conversation when they refer friends to your business.

With advertising rising in cost but often producing lackluster results, referrals are one of your best and most cost-effective marketing tools. To quote Matt Zagula again, "It's a gigantic mistake…to not use a book as a power referral tool." So, why not contact us by visiting **advantagefamily.com/finance**? We'll be happy to show you how referrals are just one of the many ways to grow your business—and your income—with a book.

CHAPTER 4

Get the Media Coverage and Free Publicity You Dream Of

From National TV to Local Radio— Be a Celebrity with Your Book

CHAPTER 4

Get the Media Coverage and Free Publicity You Dream Of

From National TV to Local Radio—Be a Celebrity with Your Book

Entrepreneurial financial advisors often dream about being interviewed for Fox Business, getting a profile in *Inc.* magazine, or landing the guest host spot on CNBC's "Power Lunch." Or at the very least, they may hope for features in financial industry journals or publications. They know the press is looking for story ideas and sources. In fact, radio alone airs interviews with over 10,000 people every single day. Yet for most advisors, this hope for publicity remains just a dream. Why?

The answer is simple. Sending press releases and hoping for coverage just doesn't cut it anymore. The media is inundated with press releases every day. Yet most of what they see is the same old thing. Most folks don't realize the media is *not* interested in them. They care only about delivering solid content to their readers, viewers, or listeners. If you want to stand out, you have to give the media something new or a great story to talk about. A book does this, and more.

When you're an author, you are considered an expert. As Mike Canet says, "a book creates that aura of celebrity, credibility, and expertise." Reporters love interviewing credible experts for content whether for radio, TV, print, or online. It makes their job easier because they can develop a story faster. Mike, by the way, has had interviews on Fox News, ABC, CNBC and several radio stations. He has also been featured in *Forbes* magazine, *USA Today*, the *Wall Street Journal* as well as in numerous local newspapers, and online publications.

He recently told me, "The results have been absolutely phenomenal. I've been in hundreds of journals and periodicals and every major station across the country. I mean, I'm just everywhere because the starting point was the book, and the book was a catalyst for all those other things."

This happens with many Advantage authors, including Thomas Helbig. Thomas reports that he has appeared on ABC, NBC, CBS and Fox affiliates around the country. Like Mike, his advice also appears in articles run by *Forbes* magazine, the *Wall Street Journal*, and *USA Today*. As he says, "The book was the start, and everything has gone from there."

Even with highly targeted audiences, a book is invaluable in securing media exposure, as Ann Vanderslice has experienced. All of her media exposure is focused in the federal arena, which is precisely where she wants it. The result, as she told me, is "a definite increase in brand recognition among federal employees."

Brian Fricke's book also generates publicity, much like the authors I've described above. However, he has also reached reporters through a different route. His book title, *Worry Free Retirement*, was an easy find for reporters using "retirement" in their online searches. The subtitle, *Do What You Want, When You Want, Where You Want*, made Brian and his book even more intriguing. As a result, he snared interviews with the Fox Business website as well as *Smart Money* magazine.

A book generates publicity for anyone, in any profession, even for people who appear not to need it. Advantage author Steve Sax is a great example of this. After retiring from 18 years in baseball, Steve was a contributing analyst for Fox Sports Prime Time. He has also appeared as a guest star on several television shows. You would think it would be easy for him to get publicity for anything he does.

However, when Steve wanted to promote his speaking and coaching business, he decided to write a book. It was a wise decision. Although he published *Shift: Change Your Mindset and Change Your World* in 2009, Steve continues to enjoy regular radio and TV interviews about his book to this day. He recently told me, "My book has been a great lead generator and a source of free publicity. And it's been good for sales, too."

Matt Dicken has also leveraged media coverage to secure more clients. Now, Matt could be considered a local media star. His TV show, *Strategic Wealth*, runs every Sunday morning on the local ABC affiliate. He also hosts *The Matt Dicken Show* for one hour every Saturday on a regional radio news talk channel. With both of these shows, Matt has the opportunity to tell viewers and listeners to contact him for an appointment. However, he does something far more powerful. He promotes his book on both shows, offering a signed copy to the first 10 people who call in. By doing this, he creates urgency. And the people who call are definitely solid leads for his business. In fact, he says new clients will often mention how they got the book.

Now, like any good marketer, Matt changes his call-to-action to something different in order to keep his offer fresh. He promotes other things on his shows, such as free reports or guides. However, Matt says, "Whether they know it or not, they will also get a copy of the book because there really isn't anything better to promote me and my business."

Thomas Helbig doesn't have his own show, but by working with someone who does, he also generates leads. Thomas has partnered with Peter D'Arruda, a financial advisor also known as "Coach Pete," whose weekly radio show airs on stations across the country. As he should, Pete rotates various offers at the end of each show, one of which is a free copy of Thomas' book. Thomas recently told me that "we get a lot of business from this, so it's definitely helping with new clients."

You can generate plenty of new leads through a local TV or radio show, or by following Thomas' method of working with another host. In fact, several Advantage authors have used their books to broker these kinds of deals. However, this is only one way to generate new business. Matt offers this advice for anyone thinking about writing a book: "Even if you don't have the TV show, I think being an author is a big step in the right direction towards really differentiating yourself. You'll stand out in the sea of sameness with all the other advisors that are out there." I couldn't have said it better.

No matter what your goal, a book has phenomenal power to get you not only in front of the media but to use this exposure for your greatest benefit. Think of the business you'll get when you're a columnist in your local newspaper. Imagine the exposure to potential clients when a superstar blogger features your book. From niche publications to national TV, a book unlocks media doors.

Whether you're a published author or just starting to write, it's never too late—or early—to plan for media coverage through your book. We can help you get the media exposure you dream of, as we have with hundreds of authors. Take the first step by visiting **advantagefamily.com/finance**.

CHAPTER 5

From $50,000 to Over $1 Million in New Annual Business

How a Book Makes It Easier to Attract New Clients and Increase Revenues

CHAPTER 5

From $50,000 to Over $1 Million in New Annual Business

How a Book Makes It Easier to Attract New Clients and Increase Revenues

Generating leads or attracting new customers is something any business owner must do—myself included. Unfortunately, many business owners are trying the same tactics as everyone else. The result is often a disappointing trickle of new leads that you have to work *hard* to sell your services to. Wouldn't it be nice to attract new prospects who are interested and *ready* to do business with you? And to have that incoming flow of prospects be more like a torrent rather than a trickle?

Advantage authors use their books to generate not only a volume of new leads but also *qualified* leads: clients they want to work with who will pay the fees they demand. And they do this using a variety of methods from the simple to complex, with increasingly impressive revenues as a result.

Take Brian Fricke for example. I've provided several examples of how Brian uses his book to generate new business. At last count, Brian had obtained five new clients *directly* from the book. While that may not sound like much, one client is worth $10,000 annually to Brian. Multiply that by five, and you have $50,000 per year in new revenues. Multiply that by the number of years Brian will likely serve these clients, and you can see how high this figure will climb.

The number of ways you can use a book to acquire clients is limited only by your imagination. You can hold a client appreciation party and provide complimentary copies of your book as parting gifts. You can personally deliver or mail a copy of your book to your best potential clients. Or you can send your book to the most influential companies and people in your industry.

This is what Chris Abts, President of Cornerstone Retirement, plans to do. Chris is going to send copies to allied professionals, such as CPAs or attorneys, with the goal of opening doors. This strategy is a good one. Mike Canet recently used his book in a campaign to secure referral partnerships with CPA firms. As a result, they now "refer business back and forth" with three CPAs. This provides new leads for his business that he wouldn't have had otherwise.

Dan Kennedy encourages advisors to use direct mail to reach ideal customers. He recently provided me with this example: "If I was a financial advisor, and I was going to do direct mail in a market area, I would take my demographic prospect list and cross it with the Levenger catalog buyer list, which are all real book people. I'd then take the affluent, the right age, and the right net worth out of the Levenger lists. I'd be happy to pay five, six times as much to get those names because they're going to value a book. They're probably going to read a book."

Think of what would happen if you sent your book to these perfect prospects. Just one new client from this list could more than pay for your campaign. Marty Higgins recognizes this opportunity. Although he is still in the process of publishing his book, he is already working on the list for his direct mail campaign. As Marty told me, "I want to use it as a credibility tool to get our ideal clients ... to reach the centers of influence."

Lead-generating campaigns range from the simple to the complex, as I mentioned earlier. One of the most sophisticated examples I have seen is the campaign implemented by Matt Zagula and Dan Kennedy, using their jointly written *Creating Trust* book.

Creating Trust was written for an exact purpose. Since it was aimed at financial advisors, it's possible you may have read it. While it provided helpful advice on establishing trust with clients, it was also a tool to fill seats at a two-day event. This event ultimately led to a two-year coaching program. I've listed the major campaign steps below.

- Their first step was to run an ad offering a free copy of the book in *Insurance News Net* magazine.

Known as an advertorial, this type of ad reads more like an article. Stuck to the ad was a removable card that opened to reveal several benefits found in the book.

- Readers were asked to call a toll-free number or to visit a landing page where they had to provide both contact information as well as stats on their business.
- Since Matt and Dan had a specific client in mind, they sent a copy of the book along with an invitation to the event to anyone who qualified, based on the information they provided. The remaining responders received a digital copy of the book by email.
- From a magazine circulation of approximately 74,000, they received over 2,800 replies.
- From the two-day Build a Better Business event, Dan and Matt developed a coaching group of 60 financial advisors, which continued for over two years.

This is probably one of the most advanced methods of using a book for direct response that I have ever come across. While it was very involved, it resulted in a seven-figure annualized business for a few years. An outstanding success! However, you may be thinking, "This must be a one-in-a-million result," or "I wouldn't want to run a campaign of this size!" Either way—the good news is you can generate leads at a level that suits you and your business.

Mike Canet is just one of countless Advantage authors who has done this. I think he summed it well when he told me, "In the last two years my business has almost doubled, and my book was the genesis of all the stepping stones along the way."

Imagine doubling your business in two years. I've only listed a few of the ways to generate new leads for your business. The Advantage team can work with you to develop even more. After all, helping you write and publish your book is only the beginning. We'll help you create a solid plan to ensure your book achieves your goals. Interested? Contact us by visiting **advantagefamily.com/finance**. Take the first step to more qualified leads for your business and higher income for you.

CHAPTER 6

How to Leverage Your Marketing Dollars

Use a Book to Reach More Prospects and Get a Better Rate of Return

CHAPTER 6

How to Leverage Your Marketing Dollars

Use a Book to Reach More Prospects and Get a Better Rate of Return

After 20 years, Ron Ware decided it was his turn.

As the President of Wealth Impact Partners, he had seen, firsthand, how books build a business. In fact, he had used several, written by various authors, to help grow his own business. However, after witnessing the power of books authored by others, Ron decided it was time to get the full benefit.

This is why Ron teamed up with Greg Hammond, President of Hammond Iles Wealth Advisors, to write their book, *You Can Do More That Matters*. As Ron said, "I've leveraged other people's books for almost 20 years in developing new business and client relationships. So the idea of having our own was even that much more compelling."

Ron knows that a book is not only the most powerful marketing tool in an entrepreneur's arsenal, it is often the most cost effective. But why?

To begin, your book is an image booster, business card, direct-response advertisement, and credibility builder *all in one.* Best of all, for less than about $5 per unit, your book does a lot when it comes to marketing. Your book helps people understand what you offer and why you are the better choice. This is *especially* important if you sell a complex product or service. A book is a unique and powerful tool to explain why and how your service works. You can also speak directly to the clients you *want* to attract. Your book is a direct marketing tool that generates publicity and builds credibility all at the same time.

Matt Dicken experiences this in his business. Most of his new clients read his book before meeting with him. Some buy it online and then call for a meeting. Others get their copy in the mail after booking their first appointment. Either way, the outcome is usually the same. Matt explains, "They'll quote lines in the book and recite things I talk about. Sometimes people will bring the book with them and it's highlighted or earmarked. If they've read the book and then meet with me, my job of trying to establish credibility with them is a whole lot easier."

Brian Fricke leverages his book when people approach him for a business card. When asked, Brian will respond, "I just gave my last card away. Why don't you give me your card? I'd like to send you a copy of my book and add you to my newsletter list." This is a very smart strategy. Brian not only reaches new prospects this way, he builds his list at the same time.

A book also allows you to be in multiple places at once—figuratively that is. Think for a minute about the power of multiplicity and leverage. Mass media, for example, allows you to leverage resources. Rather than speaking to people one by one, you can literally speak to thousands, even millions, of people at one time with radio and television. A book allows you to expand your audience as well.

Ron and Greg see this potential in their book. While the two advisors regularly market their services through presentations and other methods, they felt a book would "take the message we're distributing personally to a much wider audience." And to reach even greater numbers of potential clients, they plan to create both an audio and an e-version of their book.

This is another clever strategy. Many busy people, for example, struggle to find time to read. However, they are happy to listen to an audio book while driving to and from work. Audio books and e-books will definitely expand your reach.

A book also leverages the strengths of people, processes, media, and economies of scale so you can do a lot more in less time. In turn, this helps you to get more accomplished because you have more time to work on activities you value most. This is something Tim Wambach discovered when he worked with Advantage to publish *How We Roll.* Tim's book chronicles his work as a personal aide and caregiver for a young man with cerebral palsy, Mike Berkson. Actually, it's also a story of Mike's sense of humor and awe-inspiring positive attitude.

Tim's original goal was to raise awareness for people with special needs. He surpassed this goal beyond his expectations. Tim explains what happened: "With the help and support of Advantage Media Group, we have been able to spread our word to a broad audience. What started as helping Mike has turned into helping others like Mike…and the 'Keep On Keeping On Foundation' was born."

That is the *power of leverage* in a book.

However, books have another power that goes well beyond other media and even great examples of direct marketing: the ability to outlast nearly any other form of messaging. Consider an advertisement on TV or radio. In 30 seconds, it's gone. Trade shows quickly become a distant memory for attendees. Magazines and direct mail are good only until tossed into the recycle bin. Your message within any of these media is like a blip on the radar screen. Here one minute, gone the next.

A book, on the other hand, stands the test of time. Our society's reverence for books means we don't throw them away. Instead, we develop libraries, or share our books with others. The result brings longevity for both your book and your message.

I know authors who have used the same book, or its updated editions, to build their business for 5, 15, even 25 years. And those books are still going strong! This is why many authors update their books, or better yet, write more than one. They know how effective books are in keeping you ahead of your competition.

Ann Vanderslice summed it well when she said, "I pay attention to what my competition is doing, but as long as I keep writing books and get recognition in the places where federal employees look, they can't catch me."

If you want to take your business to the next level, you need to work smart, not just hard. After all, when it comes to running a business, small, lean entrepreneurial organizations cannot afford mistakes in marketing. A book allows you to multiply and leverage your marketing, as well as your message and image.

At Advantage, we understand that marketing is the lifeblood of your business, while spending smart is the glue that holds everything together. This is why we offer a range of services at different price levels to help you plan and write your book, as well as market and monetize it. Find out how we can help put your ideas in print by contacting us at **advantagefamily.com/finance**.

CHAPTER 7

Find Prospects Who Are Ready to Buy *Without* Salespeople

How Your Book Uncovers Untapped Markets and New Customers

CHAPTER 7

Find Prospects Who Are Ready to Buy *Without* Salespeople

How Your Book Uncovers Untapped Markets and New Customers

Would you be interested in a proven way to get new clients without spending a lot of time and money promoting your business?

As an entrepreneur, you know that new customers are your livelihood. And while it would be great to have a dedicated sales force to drum up new clients, for most small businesses this just isn't possible. Yet the challenge remains. How do you spread your message and find new clients without sales staff?

The answer lies in a "virtual sales force," which a book provides at a much lower cost than other methods.

With a book, you essentially multiply yourself, reaching far more people than ever before. In fact, your clients will often help you. Federal employee benefits expert Ann Vanderslice has experienced this first-hand. She recently told me, "My clients will get the book and then tell their co-workers, 'Oh, you've got to read this book.' I've even had one woman at the US Mint buy at least a dozen copies. She pays me for them, and then she resells them at work."

Now *that's* an avid fan and a great example of a "virtual sales force." Yet authors experience another important benefit.

When readers open your book, it's as if you're sitting across the table from them. You engage in a personal conversation with them just as a salesperson would. More importantly, when a customer or prospect is reading your book, they are focusing solely on you and your message.

This is exactly what Matt Zagula achieved with his book, *Invasion of the Money Snatchers*, which he wrote to grab the attention of a specific crowd. As you may have guessed, his target is older, conservative Americans worried about overtaxation, excessive regulations, and an unresponsive Wall Street.

Matt developed his book with this audience in mind. "There's a different conversation going on in the minds of certain consumers. So, ultimately, we wrote a message that resonated with certain belief systems." Now, you will lose some customers with this type of campaign. However, this was just fine with Matt since his goal was to resonate with his "avatar consumer," the perfect picture of his ideal client.

By entering a conversation already occurring in his prospect's mind, Matt effectively targeted his message. His next step was to leverage his "virtual sales force" by promoting his book in a TV infomercial. This is how it worked, in summary:

- Matt hired a professional spokesperson, Patty Gerbow, to conduct the interview for the infomercial.
- They ran the infomercial on the Fox network, to target his intended conservative prospects.
- They made the call-to-action for the book more enticing by noting it was an "exclusive offer for Fox viewers."
- When viewers visited the website or called the toll-free number, they heard Patty's voice again, congratulating them on their decision to get the book. This kept the campaign consistent.
- As a bonus, viewers also received a copy of Matt's "Consumer Guide." Matt includes this because "the book provides all our core values while the 'Consumer Guide' is more like a brochure."

The campaign results were incredible, to say the least. Matt was surprised to uncover "a niche market that we weren't aware of." This market becomes more apparent when you consider that calls to the toll-free line outnumbered online requests by a ratio of almost five to one. Callers tend to be elderly people who were affluent but often homebound. They are worried about their investments as well as growing regulations. This is why Matt's message connected so strongly with them. Response was significant, as a result. In some months, the campaign's rate of return was as high as 30 to 1.

Matt Zagula's extraordinary success was, in part, due to another powerful aspect of books. Books allow you to discuss the conflicts and problems your readers face in an open and nonthreatening way. You no longer have to make the typical advertising claim that your service is superior to all others. Instead, you hold a conversation with your reader, recognizing issues, establishing solutions, and showing how your philosophy, service, or product solves their problem.

This is the type of conversation Jeannette Bajalia has in her book, *Wise Up Women! A Guide to Total Fiscal and Physical Well-Being*. As she told me, her book "is for women who essentially want to take charge of their financial futures and be empowered with information." By sharing her beliefs and providing solutions, Jeannette forms a bond with her clients, often before they even step into her office.

With a book, you create a mindset in your readers. They no longer need your sales message *because they've already bought into your viewpoints and services*. After reading your book, they arrive pre-sold and ready to work with you.

Matt Dicken calls this phenomenon "salesmanship in print," and it has helped him to secure unexpected clients. In one example, Matt recently had a call from a man in Wisconsin who read his book after finding it online. He now wants Matt to handle his investments—even though Matt is located in Kentucky.

Mike Canet has had similar experiences, although he has a creative way of generating them. When traveling, Mike will leave a few copies of his book in the bestseller area of local bookstores. An unusual method, perhaps, but it works. Mike gets calls from people across the country who are interested in his advice.

A book is a cost-effective, “virtual sales force” that opens the doors to new leads. Savvy authors also include direct response techniques, bounce-backs, and special offers *within* their book to keep the phone ringing. If you’re not sure how to do this for your business, don’t worry. We can show you how to make your book a “virtual sales force,” while keeping your message and philosophies intact. To find out how, contact us at **advantagefamily.com/finance**.

CHAPTER 8

Are You Reaching Your Target Audience?

Finally—Cut Through the Noise and Influence Prospects

CHAPTER 8

Are You Reaching Your Target Audience?

Finally—Cut Through the Noise and Influence Prospects

Close your eyes for a moment and picture your top prospect. The CEO of a medium-sized enterprise has just settled into his seat on a flight from JFK to LAX. He rummages through his briefcase to find something to read. Among the papers and folders, his hands land on something solid. It's your book. He thinks to himself, "This is the perfect time to look through this." With that, he opens your book and begins to read. You now have his nearly undivided attention for the next five hours.

As a society, we are overloaded with information from email, TV, radio, and online sources. With the average American exposed to over 3,000 unique marketing messages every day, it seems almost impossible to grab the undivided attention of your prospect or client.

Fortunately, a book whisks your prospects away from this bombardment of information. They can relax and enjoy a type of stimulation they simply can't get from other media. Jay Sterling is a professional speaker and the author of Advantage title *The Other Side of Vision*. I think he summarizes this benefit perfectly: "In the same way that people often prefer reading a book to watching its movie version, a book allows our minds to escape into many arenas that the silver screen can actually limit. Even returning to some of my own writings can sometimes act as a catalyst for new and more creative thinking."

Think back for a moment to your prospect, reading your book during his flight. He is giving you his complete attention. Buying this time would be almost impossible. Even if you were a top-notch salesperson, it would take a lot of work just to get a half-hour meeting. **With your book, you have jumped to the front of the line and captured his interest.**

This alone makes publishing a book worthwhile. Yet a book cuts through the noise of competition in another way, too. If you're courting a new, potential client, think of how you'll stand out when you send her a copy of your book. Anyone in the GKIC universe calls this is a "shock and awe" package. Dan Kennedy sends his books regularly to prospects because he has witnessed, first-hand, how books generate far greater response than brochures or other literature. Matt Zagula uses this technique as well. Depending on the prospect, he may send a hard-cover book to add an element of exclusivity.

Chris Abts plans to use the "shock and awe" element of his book in yet another way: to open doors of large businesses where he can speak to employees who are close to retirement. This is exactly the audience he wants to reach. As a special bonus, he can reinforce his message by providing copies of his book to attendees.

Writing a book provides one more bonus that many would-be authors haven't considered. As an entrepreneur, you are a visionary. However, communication is the crucial link between vision and execution. Unless you can communicate your vision to clients, employees—and most importantly—to *yourself*, your venture, no matter how inspired, will never succeed. To cut through the clutter, you and your stakeholders must be clear on your vision.

While effective communication requires several components, entrepreneurs should begin with the most critical, which is your message. You must translate your vision into a clear and compelling message, and a book is the best medium to do this. Ron Ware agrees. "It's an incredible opportunity to further crystalize the message that you have, that's unique within your world or industry. And for [Greg and me], it has really honed our ability to articulate our message much more clearly and much more compellingly."

For Matt Dicken, a clear message helps to reduce another source of competition. As an advisor, he is constantly fighting the "advice" his clients or prospects get from "their next-door neighbor or an uncle who is a CFO and 'really smart with his money.'" However, after getting his book into the hands of clients, the number of times he hears these types of comments has dropped dramatically. He recently told me, "Now, pretty much whatever I recommend is what the client does. I don't get a lot of pushback. And I think a lot of it has to do with the fact that they've read my book. Even if they didn't read it, it doesn't matter. It still is a really impressive thing they have received from me. And their next-door neighbor doesn't have a published book on retirement planning. So, it kind of eliminates all the noise they're hearing, and they just focus on me and the advice I give."

For Jeannette Bajalia and Ann Vanderslice, books are a medium to broadcast messages in very specific niches. Their titles alone speak volumes. When you see *Wise Up Women! A Guide to Total Fiscal and Physical Well-Being*, you instantly know whether this book is for you. The same holds true with Ann's book, *FedTelligence: The Ultimate Guide to Mastering Your Federal Benefits*. Both books speak directly to their preferred prospects, creating an open invitation for people who need the information they provide.

A book connects you with prospects in a way that no other medium can. Your message is organized with clarity and focus. You gain the aura of being an author. As a result, your influence increases, catapulting you above your competition as never before.

If you have an idea for your book, but don't know where to begin, consider our *Fast Start Author Program*™. With this program, you'll work with our team to develop a complete, organized outline of your ideas, ready for translation to a book. From here, you can continue on to the ultimate benefits of publishing your book. Take the first step today by contacting us at **advantagefamily.com/finance**.

CHAPTER 9

Your Vehicle to Create an Impact While Increasing Your Income

Parlay Your Message into Business Success

CHAPTER 9

Your Vehicle to Create an Impact While Increasing Your Income

Parlay Your Message into Business Success

Let's face it, your message, in the right person's hands at the right time, can change that person's life. Your knowledge can pull someone out of debt, allow them to retire, or make a difference between a profitable business and bankruptcy. **Whatever your message may be, there are people eager to read it.**

You're in business because you have something unique to share with others, whether it's stories, passion, knowledge, or all three. A book manifests this information in one place. It allows you to share your vision on a far-reaching scale. When this happens, you not only have opportunities to expand your business, you have opportunities to help others while doing so.

This is one reason Marty Higgins decided to write a book. Over the years, Marty had observed that many people after retirement continue to manage their funds just as they had while working. He believes that many retirees "don't understand that tools and strategies have to be different if they want to safeguard their money."

So, Marty provided examples and strategies in his book to help readers ensure their money lasts. By sharing his message in a book, Marty believes he can help more people enjoy a long, worry-free retirement.

A book also provides an opportunity to extend your impact beyond one audience. This is what Greg Hammond and Ron Ware hope to do. Although owners of separate financial planning firms, Greg and Ron both focus on enabling people to give more to their favorite charities. After meeting through a group called the Donor Motivation Program, both agreed they had a similar message to share. Thus, plans for their joint book came to be.

Of course, they are targeting prospective clients who resonate with their message and who will want to work with their firms. However, Ron notes that "we also have a unique ability in that we have three end users of our book that potentially generate business for us in different ways." So, in addition to generating new clients directly, they see their book as a tool for nonprofits to encourage planned giving with their donors. Beyond this audience, Ron says "we also envision ourselves as becoming influencers in our industry to get more advisors thinking about doing more with clients in the way of holistic and philanthropic planning."

So, Greg and Ron hope to influence the financial industry with a book. To quote Ron again: "We're hopeful that we'll be able to utilize our book, not only to generate business, but also to make an impact both in the nonprofit industry as well as in the financial services industry." Thanks to their book, chances are high they will achieve this goal.

Sharing your message in a book provides another direct benefit. **By letting your personality shine through, you will more easily attract your ideal client.** Mike Canet once told me that before his book, a normal interaction with potential clients was a "presentation." When someone came in for their first meeting, he'd wear his "problem-solving and sales hats" in the hope of spurring interest in working with him.

However, since his book, this interaction has changed for the better. A first-time appointment with a client is no longer a presentation, but rather a meeting to share like interests. The "sales hat" is gone because it's no longer needed. As Mike said, "When people get the book and read it, they'll say, 'Hey, I liked what your book said and I want to interact with you more.' That's a pretty good feeling because it means your philosophy and beliefs resonated with somebody else."

This has been Brian Fricke's experience, as well. He explains it this way: "We run what I call a 'lifestyle business.' The purpose of our business is to facilitate a lifestyle that we envision for ourselves. We don't want our business to control our lives. So one of our philosophies is, if we're going to work, we might as well work with people we enjoy being around and working with." Brian believes his book has played a major role in making this vision possible.

For business partners Jeannette Bajalia and Brian Mickley, a book makes it easier to implement their business vision. Jeannette explains that "as a faith-based company, we are very focused on educating first." A book is an excellent way to accomplish this.

Jeannette's book trumpets her passion for ensuring that all women enjoy a healthy and dignified retirement. It allows her to address all of their needs, from financial planning to lifestyle. Equally important, it is a vehicle to share her message with others. As Brian observed, "Her book is a legacy. It's something that she's going to leave behind, that a lot of people never get around to doing."

Authors have mentioned another, often unexpected, bonus in writing a book. For many, the experience has allowed them to see their business, and even themselves, in a different light. Sometimes, it's a feeling of satisfaction, as Mike Canet has experienced. "I think that what all people want to do is say, 'I'm a published author.' So, the fact that I actually did write a book is pretty nice. It makes you feel good. It's also great for the ego."

For Thomas Helbig, writing a book has meant even more. "It's given me new confidence in my business to say 'I'm a bestselling author.' I feel more confident than ever. So, the book has changed my life. It was the best thing I've ever done."

That is pretty compelling, and I admit, a benefit I hadn't considered when I founded Advantage Media Group. However, it's another illustration of how powerful sharing your message can be.

Isn't it time to put your vision in print? Let us know what you would like to do by visiting **advantagefamily.com/finance**. We will show you how sharing your message in a book can also help you grow your business and have a lot more fun while doing it.

CHAPTER 10

An Easier Way to Create New Connections and Revenue Streams

Use Your Book to Find Business Ventures and Unexpected Opportunities

CHAPTER 10

An Easier Way to Create New Connections and Revenue Streams

Use Your Book to Find Business Ventures and Unexpected Opportunities

Inventor and entrepreneur Henry Ford once said, *"Coming together is a beginning; keeping together is progress; working together is success."* A bold statement? Perhaps. But it certainly illustrates the power of networking. It gives credence to the old saying, "It's not what you know, it's *who* you know."

Networking is essential for most professionals, including financial planners. Most will agree; networking can develop relationships that reel in new clients as well as business projects. In spite of this, many people feel that networking is too costly or takes too much time and effort. And they are often right, especially if you go about it in the traditional way.

However, a book provides a networking shortcut. Since it allows you to declare your business philosophies and solutions to specific problems, you have the ability to link with people who share your beliefs or need your answers. And some of these people will view you as an ally or potential business partner. With a book, you reach people who are *predisposed* to doing business with you. This is your key to making networking easier and far more profitable.

Steve Sax calls his book "a connector for new business." As I mentioned in an earlier chapter, Steve is a retired major-league baseball player who now has a coaching and speaking business. His primary clients include professionals and companies. After his book was published, Steve has been hired to run some baseball clinics, something he never anticipated in his business model. However, it has been a fun way for him to earn extra money.

Brian Fricke's book also resulted in an unexpected business deal. An ad agency specializing in marketing and promoting senior retirement communities found Brian on the Internet, thanks to his book's title, *Worry Free Retirement*. They hired him as a guest speaker because they felt his topic would attract potential buyers and tenants. As Brian says, "They were using me as their lead generator."

However, this opened Brian's eyes to new business opportunities. He is now in the process of sending marketing materials to agencies that cater to developers of retirement communities across the country. Brian admits this was "totally off my radar. However, it got me thinking about other industries that market to the same ideal client that we do. Will they find it attractive to hire me as a speaker and give my book to their customer base, and in essence, pay me to do my own lead generation?" Not surprisingly, Brian is exploring possibilities in this area.

I've already mentioned how entrepreneurial advisors use their books to develop partnerships with CPA and law firms. Mike Canet did this and now has three CPA firms referring clients to him, and vice versa. Dan Kennedy and Matt Zagula took this strategy a step further by selling 3,000 copies of their book to a financial services company. The company then gave the book to their sales agents and brokers. Dan reminded me that the book made this partnership possible. "The company would not promote, let's say, a teleseminar or a webinar," he said. "They wouldn't promote our newsletter offer. But they did actually buy and give a book to their agents. [A book] is an opportunity to make these things happen."

Getting your book into the hands of 3,000 brokers and salespeople, now, that's the way to network! Yet there are even more ways to use your book to create income opportunities.

For some Advantage authors, selling books is an important part of their business strategy. Ann Vanderslice fits this category. She sells her book, in both the paperback and Kindle versions, in a number of venues, including Barnes & Noble and Amazon. Clients can also purchase a copy at her office, or on her website.

In addition, Ann has another important venue where she sells her books—her own presentations. She speaks about

80 times a year to large audiences of federal employees. She is paid for these presentations, and she does something that is very smart. As Ann recently told me, "Part of the deal that I always make whenever I'm presenting is that, in addition to my fee, I get to sell books from the back of the room."

By doing this, potential clients will not only hear Ann speak, they can also take her book home. So, in addition to generating extra income from book sales, Ann also furthers her relationship with audience members. And Ann has confirmed that some of these book buyers become clients.

Yet books offer another golden opportunity. You can create an information product using your book as the foundation. This usually includes a combination of:

- Turning your book into a workbook, with expanded examples and templates
- Producing an audio version of your book or a video that provides charts, graphs, and other illustrations
- Hosting online webinars or teleseminars

Matt Dicken is planning to do this with his book. While he sees it as a way to generate additional leads, he feels the greater opportunity lies in "selling it via the Web or using different ways to get it out there where people can buy it."

Matt is 100 percent correct in trying this strategy. **Dozens of Advantage authors have added significantly to their bottom line by turning books into information products.**

And Greg Hammond and Ron Ware have yet another money-making idea that few authors consider.

Greg and Ron are planning to get a corporate sponsor to purchase thousands of their books on behalf of a nonprofit organization. The nonprofit can then give a free copy to every donor. There are several potential winners in this scenario. Donors benefit from sound financial advice that allows them to make an even greater impact by giving more. The nonprofit has an opportunity for a significant increase in gifts. The corporation scores with publicity generated by supporting a good cause. And, of course, Greg and Ron benefit from increased exposure and book sales, along with the satisfaction of connecting a nonprofit to more donations.

There are partnerships and opportunities waiting for you that you have likely never thought of. A book connects you to people who are ready to work with you, unlike traditional networking that relies on you hunting for clients. Better yet, a book provides a portal to unexpected partnerships and opportunities.

I like how Ron Ware put it when he said, "Our book has expanded our horizons big time in terms of how we can not only build our core businesses, but also in how we can develop opportunities that are way out of the box for us compared to our traditional world. And quite frankly, without our book, we may not have discovered some of these things."

It's *your* turn to open doors to new clients, business partnerships, information products, sponsors, *and new income.* When you contact us by visiting **advantagefamily.com/finance**, we'll show you how you can write a book that creates these opportunities for your business.

CHAPTER 11

Finally—Seminars That Attract Ideal Clients

How to Appeal to Affluent Prospects

CHAPTER 11

Finally—Seminars That Attract Ideal Clients

How to Appeal to Affluent Prospects

If there is one marketing tactic that nearly every financial advisor has tried, it's the seminar. And while it does generate some leads, there are also major problems with this approach.

I think Brian Fricke captured the feelings of many in the financial industry when he said, "They are horrifically expensive, time consuming, and people are often concerned about just having another insurance annuity product presentation." In other words, seminars fall into the category of "here we go again" marketing. And they are definitely less effective.

So, is there a way to make financial service seminars more intriguing and thus, more successful? A book provides not just one, but several ways to do this.

Advantage author and expert speaker Jay Sterling maintains that a book, by itself, benefits any professional who speaks, whether for an hour-long keynote or a 10-minute presentation. **Like many authors, Jay finds that his book "creates an unspoken excitement and intrigue" before he even steps on stage.** Books not only serve as a tease for your live presentation, they offer an extension of the information and experience you've shared after your event is over.

This is why Dan Kennedy pioneered the concept of an "evening with the author." Compare how you feel when you hear this versus "free seminar." If you're like most people, an "evening with the author" immediately generates a more relaxed feeling along with an element of exclusivity. Meeting with the author in a bookstore or a coffee shop has, as Dan says, a "less threatening feel to it." Interested people are also more likely to bring a spouse or a friend because, as Dan points out, "an evening with an author has a different feel than bringing them to a free workshop. Not that it's bad, but this is another way to play that has status, exclusivity, and a different appeal to different prospects."

An "evening with the author" also works well because it is *different*. Matt Dicken believes this is a major reason for the successful evenings he has hosted. "We're recycling a lot of the same ideas within our industry as far as marketing, but when you put "author" on your ad, show your book, or offer it as a free giveaway, it sets you above the rest and makes you stand out."

When the title of your book resonates with your target audience, you attract more top prospects. Jeannette Bajalia experiences this when she includes photos of her book in seminar invitations. Her business partner, Brian Mickley, commented, "I think it lends her credibility and causes some women who wouldn't have otherwise responded to the invitation to respond."

I also like Brian Fricke's twist on these events. He has promoted some of his "author evenings" as an opportunity to provide "input on our research for a potential second book." He feels this is "more interesting for people—a better hook." And since Brian is considering a second book (and all authors should!) this is a great way to check your advice and examples.

Brian has leveraged his book to secure other types of speaking opportunities. In one example, after reading his book, a manager in a local Fortune 500 company invited Brian to speak to 80 people in her department. Instead of paying a speaking fee, the company purchased copies of his book at a 50 percent discount. So, 80 people not only heard Brian that day, they also walked away with his book. About a year later, the event organizer became a client in his firm. As Brian told me, "I know I covered the cost of my book investment with that one client alone."

Brian is using a key marketing tactic. Some organizations simply do not have budgets for speaking fees. However, they do have budgets for educational materials. Books fit this category perfectly. In fact, I would argue that you're getting a much better deal than an outright fee. When you're finished speaking, your book will be in the hands of 50, 100, or even more people. They will read it and pass it on to friends and colleagues. You gain a much larger audience than you would have by simply speaking to the group for a fee.

Brian's speaking example also illustrates how, by working with organizations and companies, a professional gains access to new clients. I've seen this work for several Advantage authors, including chiropractor Dr. Scot Gray.

His book makes it easy for him to contact companies, hospitals, and community organizations because he has a "reason why" they should listen to him. "I tell them my book teaches people how to eliminate pain and have better quality of life and that I want to share these principles. It's a far better approach than just saying I want to talk to people about back pain." His method certainly works as he speaks about once every week.

Scot typically provides lectures at no cost. In fact, he offers his book as a free bonus for people who attend. He has found that "people like books, so they often come to my talk primarily to get my book." In addition, being an author provides the "credibility that many people need before they will work with me." It has been very successful; he reports he typically recruits at least one new patient at every speaking session. This is big money for Scot. On average, one patient generates $1,200 to $1,500 per year. One person per week, multiplied by $1,200 or $1,500 over 52 weeks, translates into $62,400 to $78,000 in new annual income. Not a bad way to build a profitable practice!

Advisor Mike Canet has yet another interesting way to escape the "free workshop" merry-go-round. Using his book as the foundation, Mike has developed a 150-page workbook that expands on his concepts. When he promotes his workshops, he offers both a copy of his book and the workbook. Mike then goes a step further by screening prospects who respond to his advertisements. If they meet his criteria, he then extends an invitation, sending his book along with other documents, before they attend.

By the time people arrive at his workshop, "they've been screened and processed so much, they're pretty much a done deal." As he says, "I have less people coming to my workshops, so I have fewer people coming into my office but because of that, I close a greater ratio of the people who come in." And for those prospects who decide not to work with Mike, they have all the details they need in the workbook to implement his advice on their own.

As you can see, there are several ways you can use a book to attract your ideal clients. Exclusive "evenings with the author" as well as speaking engagements with Fortune 500 companies are only some of the opportunities. I would be happy to tell you more, but you need to take the first step by contacting us at **advantagefamily.com/finance**. Don't hesitate. As Jay Sterling says, "A book will continue to pay great dividends in ways you have yet to discover."

CHAPTER 12

How to Write a Book —Quickly and Easily— on an Entrepreneur's Schedule

You Can Be a Published Author Even if You're Not a "Born Writer"

CHAPTER 12

How to Write a Book —Quickly and Easily— on an Entrepreneur's Schedule

You Can Be a Published Author Even if You're Not a "Born Writer"

In 2011, Thomas Helbig was a busy, "struggling" financial planner in St. Louis, Missouri. You may know what this is like. His days were crammed with client meetings, phone calls, and follow-up. He had to keep track of Wall Street, new regulations, an office, and staff. And if this weren't enough, he was trying to promote his business in a commoditized industry where financial planners are found on nearly any street corner.

Today, Thomas is still a busy financial planner. However, he is also a bestselling author. Within months of publishing his book, his credibility as a financial planner soared. He is now taking on "only the more valuable clients." He has "doubled his income in one year" and profits continue to climb. Best of all, he is no longer struggling.

Thomas set a new course for his business, thanks to a book that he wrote and published in the span of a few months. And he accomplished this with little impact on his day-to-day activities—or his spare time.

So how did he do it?

Thomas literally *talked* his way through his book, thanks to Advantage Media Group's unique *Talk Your Book*™ program.

Talk Your Book™ is a practical approach to authoring that has revolutionized book publishing for busy professionals and business owners. In addition to saving valuable time, it plays to your strengths, even when writing feels like a chore or you don't know where to begin.

This is why Thomas chose to "talk" his book. He recently told me, "I didn't know where to start; I'm not a born writer. Advantage said if I have a seminar, I could speak it and they could turn that into a manuscript. I do a seminar every month, and I know the subject so well, it made sense."

Chris Abts knows how much time it can take to write a book after watching his father, a *New York Times* best-selling author. This is why he decided to use the *Talk Your Book*™ program. "I saw the work and the years that my dad put in, and I recognized this was an easier way to put my thoughts on paper and to turn them into a book without a tremendous amount of effort."

***Talk Your Book*™ works because you control your message while an Advantage editor helps create and edit your text.** We make it a point to partner you with a dedicated project editor with a background that works for your book, your business, and your ideas. Your book then begins to take shape following an outline that you help create.

Even if you have a fairly detailed outline in mind, this process is helpful, according to Greg Hammond. "We had a pretty clear vision of our message and what we wanted to communicate. So, I think our outline was a little more detailed and thorough. But having the editor walk through it with us definitely flushed out a lot of good ideas."

Once your outline is complete, it's time to get your message on paper. You simply "talk" your book in a series of recorded telephone conversations with your editor, following the outline you both created. Your editor will schedule times that work for you.

Advantage author Robert Phelan, decided to write his book this way. After his experience, Robert told me, "I give two thumbs up for your *Talk Your Book*™ program. I simply talked for eight hours, and your team turned it into a book. It was easy and enjoyable."

Ann Vanderslice completed the program from the comfort of her office. "Advantage made the process easy. They laid out exactly what I had to do. They set up the phone calls, and all I had to do was get on them and talk. It was a great experience. I am sure I wouldn't have written the book in that timeframe without them."

No matter which method you choose, your project editor will harvest and edit the resulting transcripts. These eventually become your first rough draft. You'll then have several opportunities to edit your book, making sure it says what you want it to say, in your words. Mike Canet summarized his experience this way: "I literally just had to talk and share my thoughts and feelings and my editor made sure they were cohesive. It makes sense on paper, and when you read it, they are my words."

Next, you collaborate with our design experts to develop a cover and interior layout. Finally, after we have your stamp of approval, your book goes to press. Before you know it, copies will arrive at your door. The process couldn't be easier, which appealed to Ron Ware and Greg Hammond. Ron commented that, "One of the things that appealed to us was the defined process. We're both process guys in our practices and the way we plan with our clients. So, the idea of using a process that was executable and easy to plug into, from beginning to end, was attractive."

For Matt Dicken, *Talk Your Book*™ provided an additional benefit: accountability. For him, one of the greatest benefits was "having someone help me and hold me accountable for getting it done. I'm the type of person, if I make a commitment to someone else, then I'm definitely going to make it."

However, our support doesn't end after we ship your books. At Advantage Media Group, we recognize that our success is based on your success, which is why we continue to provide support, advice, and ongoing programs to help you reach your goals—long after your book is published. Most of our authors find this to be as important as the process of publishing itself. This is what author Teri Johnson realized when publishing her book. "From the very beginning, from flushing out the ideas, and brainstorming with the team, writing the outline and talking the book, through to the day the actual book was personally delivered to my hands and after, working with the support staff—the experience was and is positive, encouraging, and enjoyable."

A book is the ultimate game-changer for your business. Advantage authors leverage their books to exponentially grow their businesses—and their incomes. This is why they will tell you not to hesitate when it comes to writing yours. Marty Higgins offers this advice: "If you've been in business for any length of time, you've got a lot of stories, examples, and analogies in your head. You just need somebody to pull it out of you. And that's what Advantage does. *Talk Your Book*™ is really a simple process."

They will also tell you it's one of the best—if not *the* best—investments they've made in their business. Yes, it takes some time and money, but author Burrow Hill summed it up this way: "As a numbers guy, I found working with Advantage to be less expensive than any other means. When I placed the appropriate hourly rate on my time and added up the time it would have cost me to: research, get proposals, evaluate and hire a self-publisher; research, get proposals, evaluate and hire editors, designers, photographers, cover designers, it was less expensive, faster, and dramatically easier to use Advantage." And I should add Burrow now calls his book "the cornerstone" of his business.

Contact us at **advantagefamily.com/finance**. We'll answer any questions you have about timing, cost, and the many options available to make your book a reality. And if you're still hesitating, consider this advice from Michael Canet: "We can all think of excuses and continue to procrastinate. I think anybody who is contemplating writing a book has been getting ready to write it for months, if not years. Just take that step forward. It's going to cost you a little bit of money, but the money is worth it in the long run. I have clearly made significant income off that first step I took."

I think this says it all. Now, it's time for *your* opportunity. Let us help you seize it. Take your first step by visiting **advantagefamily.com/finance** today.

ARE YOU READY TO ACHIEVE MORE THAN YOU EVER THOUGHT POSSIBLE?

A book is your game-changer. It's the missing link you need to accelerate your business, communicate your message, and reach your dreams.

Success from your book begins with a strong strategy, develops with experienced editing, grows with sound marketing, and takes flight with a monetization plan. At Advantage, we can help you with one or all of these steps, depending on where you are in the process. You'll be an author with a professionally published book that imparts your message to *your* audience.

ARE YOU TAKING THE FIRST STEP? NOT SURE WHERE TO BEGIN?

With our ***Fast Start Author Program***™, we'll help you develop your book strategy and editorial outline. You'll walk away with a blueprint unique to you and your business. From here, you decide on your next step, whether it's publishing with us or doing it on your own. Whatever you decide, the insight you will glean from this process will be invaluable to you even if you never write a book.

DO YOU SEE A BOOK IN YOUR FUTURE BUT WORRY ABOUT THE TIME IT WILL TAKE TO WRITE IT?

Create your book's message in a matter of hours with our ***Talk Your Book™ creation system.*** You simply speak your ideas following an outline that we create for you. Our editorial team puts your ideas on paper. You review, revise, and finally, approve your manuscript. We help you add the finishing touches, and you become a published author in just a few months!

ARE YOU READY TO PUBLISH YOUR MANUSCRIPT?

If you have a manuscript, even if it's only *partly* finished, our seasoned team will edit and polish your book with your guidance and input. We use your ideas to create a professional cover design, inviting cover copy, and custom graphics or illustrations for your book's interior. Finally, with our ***Launch Your Book™ publishing system*** we'll distribute your book to more than 25,000 bookstores and online retailers. Your life will be forever changed from this point on!

HAVE YOU INVESTED IN A BOOK BUT HAVEN'T FOUND A WAY TO KEEP THE MARKETING MOMENTUM GOING?

Our done-for-you ***Book The Business™ marketing service*** gives you the marketing tools you need to make your book a success. You simply provide us with your book or other content, and we provide the marketing tools and support. Then, watch your presence grow with ongoing marketing, speaking opportunities, and publicity.

IS IT TIME TO MAKE MORE MONEY FROM YOUR BOOK?

With our ***Monetize Your Book***™ online learning system, we help you convert your book or speeches into engaging, self-paced online courses for you to sell online. We work with you to develop a course structure, record your presentation, and monetize your course online. Before you know it, you'll be making money while you sleep.

WITH OUR HELP, IN A FEW SHORT MONTHS, YOU CAN JOIN THE RANKS OF PUBLISHED AUTHORS.

You can add this title to your biography, website, and business card. You can enjoy the benefits a book provides—from new opportunities and increased income, to free publicity and celebrity status—as hundreds of Advantage authors have.

Or, you can maintain the status quo.

The choice is yours. So why not contact us at advantagefamily.com/finance and tell us how we can help you best? Your new opportunities begin with *this* first step.

"As the person who is responsible for keeping a close eye on the finances of the company, I was skeptical about Jeannette spending money on a book. I was skeptical about the return and even more so after it was published. Then, I heard clients talking about the book. I saw the ways we could use it. And we've already paid for our investment a few times over through new clients and all the intangible benefits we've gotten from it—in the span of just over one year."

Brian Mickley

Business partner with author, Jeannette Bajalia
Petros Estate and Retirement Planning
Woman's Worth®

AND ACCESS FREE RESOURCES FOR POTENTIAL AUTHORS!

It doesn't matter where you are in the world, Adam can help you share your Stories, Passion, and Knowledge with the world in the form of a published book.

Visit HOWTOATTRACTIDEALCLIENTS.COM/REGISTER to access these free resources:

RECEIVE a subscription to the Author Success University™ monthly teleseminar wherein successful authors and book marketing experts reveal their tips and tricks for marketing and growing a business with a book

REGISTER for a webinar led by Adam Witty: "How to Quickly Write, Publish, And Profit From A Book That Will Grow Your Business"

COMPLETE Advantage's Publishing Questionnaire and receive a complimentary Discovery Call with an acquisitions editor to help you determine if your ideas, concepts, or manuscript are worth turning into a book

ACCESS ALL OF THE ABOVE FREE RESOURCES BY REGISTERING YOUR BOOK AT

HOWTOATTRACTIDEALCLIENTS.COM/REGISTER

Printed in the USA
CPSIA information can be obtained
at www.ICGtesting.com
JSHW012040140824
68134JS00033B/3165

9 781599 324548